ITEM BY ITEM

Basics...

There are several types of fresh Italian sausage. Among others, Northern Italian, Sicilian, Cotechino, and Luganega sausages are all variations made from a combination of pork and/or beef, and are distinguished by key ingredients found in them such as cheeses, parsley, cloves, orange peel, cinnamon, fresh finoccio and wine. Additionally, in some instances such as Sicilian and Luganega, the sausage is stuffed into thinner diameter casings.

The most favored sausages, and the best-suited for cooking recipes, are mild, sweet, or hot Italian sausages, which are usually made from pure pork. Mild Italian sausage uses ground anise to achieve sweetness, while sweet Italian sausage uses sugar or dextrose to achieve sweetness. In hot Italian sausage, crushed red pepper is added for heat.

The highest quality and most flavorful Italian sausages are made with fresh Boston pork butts (an extension of the shoulder), which when trimmed to one-fourth inch layer of fat, yield about 72% to 74% lean, and give the perfect proportion of meat, fat and moisture. This meat together with salt and natural spices, which may include whole fennel seeds, pepper, whole or ground anise, nutmeg, allspice, cardamon, garlic, water and sometimes even orange peel, make the ideal combination for the best tasting Italian sausage. The sausage is then usually stuffed into natural sausage casings and twisted into links.

Italian sausage is also made from poultry meats; most commonly, turkey or chicken. These can also be obtained in mild, sweet, hot and sometimes "hot & spicy" versions. Most poultry sausages are very lean because there is no fat in the meat naturally. For this reason, it is particularly important to remember not to overcook poultry sausages, as they can easily become dry.

Lastly, Italian sausage can be made from wild game meats such as venison, wild boar, elk, and others. Wild game meats are very lean naturally, and should be cooked in the same manner as poultry products.

Making The Buy...

If buying sausage from an Italian grocer or a butcher shop, don't hesitate to ask about leanness, ingredients, and other particulars about its making. If buying sausage from a retail grocery store, read the label carefully, including ingredient information and expiration date. Make sure the product is U.S.D.A. approved. If you have any questions about store bought sausage, call the manufacturer collect. Most will welcome the inquiry, and won't mind paying for the call to tell you how their sausages are made.

Sausage can be purchased in three forms. Most often, it is sold in link form, four to five links per pound. It can also be purchased in bulk, which is perfect for some recipes and for use as pizza topping. Lastly, sausage may sometimes be found unlinked and sold in rope style.

Buy the freshest sausage available. Purchased at a butcher counter and wrapped in paper, fresh sausage will generally retain its freshness and bloom for about four to five days. Tray wrapped from a supermarket, sausage should have no more than ten days shelf life. Fresh sausage should always be used soon after purchasing, or if not, frozen, in which case it should keep its full flavor for up to forty-five days. Regardless of the packaging used, proper refrigeration is the key to shelf life.

Notes On Cooking...

As a general rule, let sausage temper for about ten minutes before cooking as putting cold sausage on a hot grill will tend to split the casings. Never poke or prick sausage before cooking as this will allow rich flavorful juices to escape the meat. Contrary to some belief, Italian sausage does not need to be par boiled before cooking.

Cooking times for sausage may vary slightly depending on the appliance used. As a rule of thumb, 325 degrees is the approximate correct heat on an electric skillet, or medium-high heat on a gas appliance.

Sausage may be cooked in any number of ways, but no matter what method is used, links will generally be cooked in about sixteen to thirty minutes, and are finished **just as the meat looses its pink color inside.**

Instead of using a fork to turn sausage while cooking, use tongs. The best tongs to use for turning sausage are the long handled, spring loaded, stainless steel type, as opposed the scissor type.

When cutting or slicing cooked Italian sausage, use a sharpened knife. A dull knife will rip the casings and not give a good clean cut.

To pan fry sausage, lightly wipe the interior of a frying pan or electric skillet with olive oil and preheat to 325 degrees or medium high heat. Cook the sausage for about fifteen to eighteen minutes, turning occasionally.

To broil sausage, preheat the broiler. Place the sausage on the broiler pan, about three to four inches from the heat source, usually second shelf from top. Broil for about sixteen to eighteen minutes, turning occasionally. In an electric oven, broil with the door ajar.

To bake sausage, preheat the oven to 350 degrees. Lightly wipe the bottom of a glass baking dish with olive oil, place the sausage in the dish, and bake for twenty-five to thirty minutes, uncovered.

To steam sausage, place the sausage in a medium-sized skillet and add eight to twelve ounces of water or other desired liquid such as chicken broth, wine, beer, etc. Cook on medium high heat, covered, for twenty to twenty-five minutes.

To Bar-B-Q sausage, mound the briquettes into a pyramid on the coal rack of the grill. Light the fire in the usual method and let kindle for about fifteen minutes until the coals become ashed over. Safely spread the coals out into a single layer. Arrange the links on the grill and cook for about twenty minutes, turning occasionally. *(Note: if cooking a large number of sausages, juices may drip onto overheated coals and cause a fire flare-up to occur. To help prevent this from happening, make sure the coals have already peaked and are not flaming before putting the sausages on. You may also want to use a grill basket, and keep a spray bottle of water handy.)*

Throughout This Book, In Using...

Olive oil, use extra virgin as opposed to virgin or pure. Because of its low acidity, it is the finest and most aromatic of all oils.

Butter, use the highest grade, unsalted, as it is usually fresher and has a better taste.

Garlic, one teaspoon of chopped, crushed or minced garlic is equal to one to two average-sized fresh garlic cloves.

Tomatoes, the preference is *plum* tomatoes which have a meatier flesh, fewer seeds, excellent flavor, and are particularly well-suited for long cooking in sauces. Common red tomatoes are available year-round, but are more flavorful in summer. If not using fresh tomatoes, there are a variety of quality canned tomato products available. *(To peel tomatoes, bring a pan of water to a rapid boil, making sure there will be enough water to cover the tomatoes. Core out the stem end and cut an "X" in the skin on the bottom end of the tomatoes. Drop the tomatoes into the boiling water for about twenty or thirty seconds. Remove the tomatoes from the pan with a slotted spoon and run them under cold water as you peel the skin away. To seed tomatoes, cut them in half and flush out the seeds under cold running water.)*

Cooking Wine, it should also be just as suitable for drinking.

Oregano, powerful and robust, it is one of the few herbs that is more flavorful when dried.

Basil, fresh is best. When using fresh basil, do not wash the leaves, simply wipe them off with a moist cloth. *(If fresh basil is hard to find, stock up when you can! Here's a great way to keep basil for months and still have it retain its wonderful fragrance when you're ready to use it. Coarsely chop the basil, and neatly put one tablespoon into each compartment of an ice cube tray. Carefully fill each compartment with water and store in your freezer. The next time you have a sauce that calls for basil, just pop in a pre-measured basil ice cube!)*

Salt, sea salt is preferred. Unlike rock salt, it contains only 34% sodium chloride.

Pepper, use freshly ground black pepper.

Pasta, choose a good quality imported or domestic dried pasta. We're particular about our sauces, and are always careful to use the right shaped pasta to hold a particular sauce.

One pound of pasta will serve about four as a main course or up to six people as a side dish. Pasta cooked to perfection takes particular care in timing. Generally speaking, bring five quarts of water to a boil, then add one tablespoon of olive oil and one tablespoon of salt. Gradually add one pound of pasta to boiling water and continue cooking at high heat, with an occasional stir. Long pastas such as linguini and spaghetti should be fed into the boiling water and not broken. Depending on the shape and size of the pasta, cooking times may vary between eight and fourteen minutes.

When the water starts to boil, don't even *THINK* about leaving the kitchen! Because of its short cooking time and necessity to be cooked just right when served, pasta should be the last part of your meal cooked, with the sauce and any accompanying side dishes just finishing. Toward the end of your cooking time, test the pasta frequently and continue cooking until it is al denté (an Italian term meaning "to the tooth"), tender, yet still firm.

Cheese, Parmesan cheese, which is made from cow's milk, and Romano cheese, made from sheep's milk with a little sharper bite, are both excellent for grating. Use a really good Parmesan cheese (Parmigiano-Reggiano is the best!) or a good, imported aged Romano cheese such as Pecorino Romano, which has a slight pepper flavor.

Simple Kitchen Math:

A "pinch" or a "dash"	=	Less than ⅛ of a teaspoon
3 teaspoons	=	I tablespoon
4 tablespoons	=	¼ of a cup
5 tablespoons and I teaspoon	=	⅓ of a cup
8 tablespoons	=	½ of a cup
10 tablespoons and 2 teaspoons	=	⅔ of a cup
12 tablespoons	=	¾ of a cup
16 tablespoons	=	I cup
2 tablespoons	=	I fluid ounce
I cup	=	½ of a pint or 8 fluid ounces
2 cups	=	I pint or 16 fluid ounces
4 cups	=	2 pints or I quart or 32 fluid ounces
4 quarts	=	I gallon
16 ounces	=	I pound

Everything You Will Need is described as it will be used in the recipe. Preparing all of the ingredients first makes the whole cooking process flow a lot easier. Organization in the kitchen is the key to success in cooking. Have a place for everything and keep everything in its place!

In all recipes, the term "fresh Italian sausage" is used. You may use any of the variety of fresh Italian sausages, however, where a particular type of sausage is mentioned, it has been found to work particularly well in that case.

Now, let's cook Italian sausage!

Papa's Special

This one is easy; a family favorite prepared many a Sunday morning by Papa himself!

Everything You Will Need:

8   fresh eggs
I   pound of fresh Italian sausage
         (removed from casings)
I½   cups of onion *(chopped)*
4   teaspoons of olive oil
I   10 ounce package of chopped, frozen
         spinach *(thawed and drained)*
         salt and freshly ground black pepper

Beat the eggs in a small bowl and set aside.

In a large skillet, cook the sausage and the onion in the olive oil for about ten to twelve minutes, stirring occasionally with a wooden spoon to crumble the sausage.

Add the eggs and spinach to the sausage and onion.

Scramble until the eggs are done.

Add salt and pepper to taste and serve hot.

(Note: For a single serving, use one-fourth of all ingredients, and cook in a small eight inch skillet).

Serves A Family Of 4 Nicely.

SAUSAGE & EGG CASSEROLE

Fresh and light, this is great for breakfast or brunch.

Everything You Will Need:

½   pound of fresh Italian sausage *(removed from the casings)*
I   tablespoon of olive oil
I   tablespoon of butter
4   slices of white bread *(crust removed)*
6   eggs
½   cup of milk
¼   teaspoon of salt
¼   teaspoon of freshly ground black pepper
¼   teaspoon of crushed red pepper
½   cup of fresh, ripe tomatoes *(diced)*
4   ounces of fresh mushrooms *(sliced)*
½   cup of fresh zucchini *(diced)*
½   cup of Monterey jack cheese *(grated)*
½   cup of cheddar cheese *(grated)*

A Day Before Serving:

In a small frying pan, cook the sausage in the olive oil over medium heat for about ten to twelve minutes, stirring occasionally with a wooden spoon to crumble the sausage.

Butter the bottom and sides of a two quart baking dish.

Line the bottom of the dish with white bread.

Spread the sausage evenly over the bread.

In a medium-sized bowl, beat the eggs, milk, salt, pepper, and crushed red pepper.

Stir into the eggs the tomatoes, mushrooms, and zucchini.

Pour the mixture over the sausage.

Top with the cheeses.

Cover the mixture and refrigerate overnight.

The Day Of Serving:

Place the casserole in the oven and bake at 350 degrees *(do NOT preheat the oven)* on the center rack for fifty-five to sixty minutes, until the edges are lightly browned and the center is set.

Serve hot.

Serves 4 For A Good Start On The Day.

SAUSAGE & TORTILLA PIE

What can we say but....Olé!

Everything You Will Need:

½ pound of fresh Italian sausage
  (*removed from the casings*)
I tablespoon of olive oil
I tablespoon of butter
6 corn tortillas (*torn into strips*)
I 8 ounce can of chopped green chilies
I½ cups of Monterey jack cheese (*grated*)
¼ cup of green onion (*chopped*)
2¼ ounces of black olives (*sliced*)
4 eggs
¼ cup of buttermilk
¼ teaspoon of crushed or chopped garlic
¼ teaspoon of salt
¼ teaspoon of freshly ground black pepper
¼ teaspoon of chili powder
¼ teaspoon of crushed chili pepper
¼ teaspoon of ground cumin
I fresh, ripe tomato (*sliced*)
  paprika
  whole black olives, sour cream, and salsa,
  (*for garnish*)

Serves 4, But Great For 8 When Doubled.

A Day Before Serving:
In a small frying pan, cook the sausage in the olive oil over medium heat for ten to twelve minutes, stirring occasionally with a wooden spoon to crumble the sausage.

Drain off any liquid and set the sausage aside.

Butter the interior of a round or square two quart baking dish.

Line the bottom and the sides of the dish with a little over one-half of the tortilla strips.

Spread one-half of the chilies evenly on top of the tortilla strips.

Spread one-half of the sausage evenly on top of the chilies.

Spread one-half of the cheese evenly on top of the sausage.

Spread one-half of the green onion evenly on top of the cheese.

Spread one-half of the olives evenly on top of the green onion.

Cover with the remaining tortilla strips.

Spread the remaining one-half of the ingredients in layers, as in the steps above.

In a small bowl, whisk together the eggs, buttermilk, garlic, salt, black pepper, chili powder, crushed chili pepper and cumin until they are blended well.

Pour the eggs over the top of the ingredients in the baking dish.

Arrange the tomato slices on top and dust over with the paprika.

Cover and refrigerate overnight.

The Day Of Serving:
Remove the covering from the baking dish.

Bake the pie at 350 degrees for fifty-five to sixty minutes *(do NOT preheat the oven)*, until the edges are lightly browned and the center is set.

Cut the pie into four servings. Top each tomato with a black olive and serve with salsa and sour cream.

EGGS IN THE HOLE

Here's our Italian version of Eggs Benedict. It's dynamite!

Everything You Will Need (Per Serving):

I	link of fresh Italian sausage
¼	cup of Italian spaghetti sauce
	(Caryn's Sunday sauce, found on page 98, is perfect for this!)
I	tablespoon of butter
2	slices of French or Italian bread
	(use a ⅜ inch thick slice from a 4¼ inch wide loaf. Cut a hole about 2½ inches in diameter in the center of each slice).
2	large eggs
I	tablespoon of Parmesan or Romano cheese *(grated)*

Pan fry or broil the sausage.

Meanwhile...
Heat the Italian spaghetti sauce, then reduce heat and cover to keep warm until serving.

Melt the butter in a frying pan over medium heat.

Put the bread in the pan, let it soak up some of the melted butter and turn it over.

Crack the eggs carefully into the hole in the center of the bread.

Raise the heat to medium-high and cook for about two minutes.

Flip the bread and eggs over with a spatula.

Cook the second side about one minute.

Place the eggs and sausage on a plate, and ladle the spaghetti sauce over the eggs.

Sprinkle the grated cheese over the top of the sauce and serve hot.

One Serving. *(multiply measures by the number of servings desired.)*

ITALIAN SAUSAGE FRITTATA

This one is tricky, but it's great fun and makes a terrific breakfast dish! (May require some practice, so try it a couple of times alone before trying to impress the family!)

Everything You Will Need:

½   pound of fresh Italian sausage
     (removed from the casings)
1½   cups of onion *(chopped)*
2½   tablespoons of olive oil
4   ounces of fresh mushrooms *(sliced)*
1   tablespoon of butter
1½   teaspoons of fresh basil leaves *(chopped)*
1   teaspoon of fresh parsley *(chopped)*
½   cup of fresh, ripe tomatoes *(chopped)*
6   fresh eggs
1   tablespoon of Half & Half
¼   cup of Parmesan or Romano cheese
     (grated)
¼   teaspoon of salt
½   teaspoon of freshly ground black pepper
¼   teaspoon of dried oregano
     a pinch of ground nutmeg

Serves 4 once you get the hang of it.

In a medium-sized skillet, cook the sausage and onion in one tablespoon of olive oil over medium heat for about six or seven minutes, stirring with a wooden spoon to crumble the sausage.

Add the mushrooms and butter.

Continue to cook for another three or four minutes.

Add the basil, parsley and tomatoes.

Cook for three or four minutes more.

Drain off any liquid and set aside.

In a medium-sized bowl, beat the eggs.

Stir into the eggs the Half & Half, cheese, salt, pepper, oregano, nutmeg, and the sausage and onion mixture.

Heat the remaining olive oil in a really good, non-stick ten to twelve inch frying pan.

Pour in the mixture.

Reduce the heat to low and cook for about fifteen to twenty minutes, or until the edges are set.

Gently lift the edges occasionally, and tilt the pan so the egg runs entirely to the sides.

Continue to cook until the eggs are almost set on top.

VERY lightly, wipe the top of a large flat plate with olive oil.

Cover the pan with the plate and carefully flip the frittata onto it.

Slide the frittata back into the pan, and finish cooking for another couple of minutes.

Place a clean plate over the pan and flip the frittata out of the pan for serving.

(As an option, instead of frying the frittata, it can be poured into a ten inch glass baking dish, lightly oiled, and baked at 350 degrees for about forty to forty-five minutes, or until the eggs are done.)

Serve hot.

SAUSAGE SANDWICHES

Few things are as savory as an Italian sausage sandwich, whether it's barbecued, broiled or pan fried. The key ingredient is a good quality Italian sausage. Choose your favorite, whether it be pork, turkey or chicken. Use a good fresh Italian or French roll, Mexican bolillo, or torpedo roll. Pick one that works nicely with the sausage you're using; so that the bread doesn't overwhelm the sausage. Cut into, but not all the way through the roll, so that the sausage will be held in it.

Here then, are some great combinations to try. If you're cooking for more than just yourself, whether it be a large or small crowd, get ready to have your ego boosted a couple of notches. Typically, "Wow! This Is Great!" or "Ahhhh!" are familiar words and sounds you'll hear after the first bite. So go ahead, ham it up a little...you deserve it!

Here are some quick and easy ideas to get you started, after that, be creative...you're on your own!

With Peppers & Onions
Barbecue, broil, or pan fry the sausage.

Clean and remove the seeds from one green bell pepper, then slice it thinly.

Slice one-half of an onion.

Cook the peppers and onions in one tablespoon of olive oil for about fifteen minutes, covered over medium heat.

Spoon peppers and onions over the sausage in your favorite roll.

(To REALLY impress, you may also want to top the sandwich with a small ladle of Caryn's Sunday sauce, found on page 98, and finish it off with some grated Mozzarella cheese).

With Tomato, Avocado & Lettuce
Barbecue, broil, or pan fry the sausage.

Spread mayonnaise and ketchup on a fresh roll, then add the sausage, sliced tomato wedges, avocado and lettuce.

With Mayo, Mustard & Peperoncini
Barbecue, broil or pan fry the sausage.

Spread mayonnaise and mustard on roll and add Italian peperoncini peppers, sliced lengthwise. Place sausage in the roll.

THE COMBINATIONS ARE ENDLESS!!!

New Orleans Style
Sausage Muffaletta Sandwich

Here's a sandwich made famous in New Orleans, distinguished by its unique olive salad, and usually stuffed into round Italian bread loaves. We added broiled Italian sausage. What an inspiration!

Everything You Will Need:

1	pound of fresh Italian sausage links
1	large loaf of Italian or French bread
4	slices of Provolone cheese
8	thin slices of Italian salami
1½	cups of New Orleans style olive salad
	(see recipe on page 101)

Broil or bake the sausage.

When the sausage is done, cut each sausage in half lengthwise.

Cut off the ends of the loaf of bread, and cut the remaining bread into four pieces, measuring about three and one-half by five inches each.

Cut each piece of bread in half.

From the top half of each piece remove a small amount of bread from the center.

On the bottom piece of each piece of bread, spoon on one tablespoon of the New Orleans style olive salad.

Now it's time to assemble the sandwiches:
Put the sausage slices on the bottom pieces of bread.

Add a slice of cheese on top.

Add two slices of salami on top of the cheese.

Spoon on one heaping mound of the olive salad.

Place the top piece of each square on its matching bottom half, and press down *(hold on and don't let go!)*.

4 Perfect Sandwiches.

STUFFED MUSHROOMS

Mouth watering appetizers that will make you the favorite person on the block!

Everything You Will Need:

½   pound of fresh Italian sausage
        (removed from the casings)
1¼ cups of onion *(finely chopped)*
1   tablespoon of olive oil
2   tablespoons of green bell pepper
        (finely chopped)
1   pound of fresh mushrooms *(medium-sized)*
        *(save the caps, remove the stems and
        chop them finely)*
1   teaspoon of salt
    freshly ground black pepper
1   3 ounce package of cream cheese
2   tablespoons of butter *(melted)*
¼   cup of Italian seasoned breadcrumbs
    fresh parsley *(for garnish)*

In a large skillet, cook the sausage and onion in the olive oil over medium heat for five to six minutes, stirring occasionally with a wooden spoon to crumble the sausage.

Add the chopped onion, green bell pepper, mushroom stems, the salt, and pepper to taste.

Continue to cook for six or seven minutes or until the onion and bell pepper are tender.

Turn off the heat and stir the cream cheese into the mixture.

Fill the mushroom caps with the sausage mixture *(approximately one teaspoon each)*.

In a small bowl, thoroughly mix the butter and the breadcrumbs.

Press the stuffed mushroom caps firmly into the buttered breadcrumbs. *(Use a teaspoon, if necessary, to help keep the mixture from falling out of the mushroom cap as you turn it over into the breadcrumbs.)*

Put two tablespoons of water into a nine inch by thirteen inch glass baking dish.

Place the mushroom caps in the dish, breaded sides up.

Preheat the oven to 350 degrees.

Bake for about twenty to twenty-five minutes, or until the breadcrumbs are browned.

Serves 8 to 10 For Appetizers, Depending On Their Appetites. (These disappear quickly!)

Sprinkle on fresh parsley and serve.

SPIEDINI

If you have the time and patience, here is one of the best tasting dishes you'll ever eat! This is my grandmother's original recipe from Villa Rosa, Sicily. A one-hundred year old family favorite!

Everything You Will Need:

3	pounds of beef round steak *(½ inch thick)*
1	tablespoon of butter
½	pound fresh Italian sausage *(removed from the casings)*
1¼	cups of onion *(finely chopped)*
1	teaspoon of crushed or chopped garlic
1½	cup of Italian seasoned breadcrumbs
½	cup of Parmesan or Romano cheese *(grated)*
2	tablespoons of fresh parsley *(chopped)*
¼	teaspoon of salt
½	teaspoon of freshly ground black pepper
1	egg *(hard boiled and grated)*
50	bay leaves
3	tablespoons of olive oil

Makes 45 to 50 Incredible Delights!

Round steak is usually about one-half inch thick. Slice the meat in half to about one-fourth inch thickness.

Pound the meat to an even thickness and cut into pieces about three and one-half inches square.

Set the steak aside.

In a medium-sized frying pan cook the onion, garlic, and sausage in the butter over medium heat for seven or eight minutes, stirring frequently with a wooden spoon to crumble the sausage.

In a medium-sized bowl, mix the breadcrumbs, grated cheese, parsley, salt and pepper.

Mix in the sausage, onion, and grated egg. *(The filling should not be too dry or too moist).*

Put about one tablespoon of filling in the center of a piece of the round steak and tightly roll it with a small overlap.

Place the spiedini on a skewer, along with a bay leaf.

Repeat the above process for the remaining pieces of steak.

Put on eight spiedini per skewer, with a bay leaf between each one.

Brush the spiedini with the olive oil.

Preheat the broiler. Broil the spiedini for six to seven minutes per side and serve hot.
.

(This is also great as a main dish served with a side of pasta!)

SAUSAGE & THREE CHEESE CROSTINI

A real treat for the taste buds!

Everything You Will Need:

½   pound fresh Italian Sausage
    (removed from casings)

½   cup of onion *(finely chopped)*

1   teaspoon of crushed or chopped garlic

1   tablespoon of olive oil

½   cup of Ricotta cheese

⅔   cup of Parmesan cheese *(grated)*

¼   cup of Provolone cheese *(grated)*

1   cup of fresh, ripe tomatoes
    (peeled, seeded and chopped)

2   tablespoons of fresh basil *(finely chopped)*

2   tablespoons of fresh parsley *(finely chopped)*

18 slices of baguette-style bread
    (cut ½ inch slices)

In a medium-sized skillet, cook the sausage, onion, and garlic in the olive oil over medium heat for six to eight minutes, stirring occasionally with a wooden spoon to crumble the sausage.

Remove the mixture and place in a medium-sized bowl. Do not drain.

Add in the Ricotta cheese, one-half of the Parmesan cheese, the Provolone cheese, the tomatoes, basil, parsley, and salt and pepper to taste and mix together.

Preheat the broiler. Place the rack six to eight inches from the heat source.

Put one tablespoon of the mixture onto each of the bread slices and sprinkle the tops with the remaining Parmesan cheese.

Place on a cookie sheet and broil for about five to six minutes *(be careful not to burn)*.

Serve hot.

Serves 8 Gourmet Appetites.

MUSHROOM & SAUSAGE TOASTS

A great appetizer for friends with style!

Everything You Will Need:

½   pound of fresh Italian sausage
    (removed from casings)
¼   cup of onion *(chopped)*
1½ tablespoons of olive oil
7   tablespoons of butter
¾   pound of fresh mushrooms *(thinly sliced)*
½   teaspoon of crushed or chopped garlic
3   tablespoons of fresh lemon juice
2   tablespoons of fresh orange juice
    salt and freshly ground black pepper
¼   cup of Italian parsley *(chopped)*
14 slices of baguette style bread
    (cut into ½ inch thick slices)

In a medium-sized frying pan, cook the sausage, onion, and garlic in the olive oil and one tablespoon of the butter over medium-high heat for ten to twelve minutes, stirring occasionally with a wooden spoon to crumble the sausage.

In another pan, melt three tablespoons of butter, and sauté the mushrooms for six to eight minutes.

When the mushrooms are finished, add them back to the sausage and onions with the lemon juice, orange juice and salt and pepper to taste. *(Save this pan; you'll need it again in a few more minutes!)*

Reduce the heat and simmer for about five minutes.

Stir in the parsley and keep warm.

Melt the remaining butter in the pan you saved.

Preheat the broiler. Place the rack six inches from heat source.

Lightly dip the bread slices in the butter, one side only.

Place the bread slices in the broiler, buttered side up, and broil until the tops begin to toast.

Remove the bread slices from the broiler and spoon the hot sausage and mushrooms on the toasts.

Let cool for a minute or two and serve warm.

Serves 6 to 8 Elegantly.

Hot & Spicy Sausage Hors D'Oeuvres

For this one, you'll only need three ingredients and it's guaranteed to be a real crowd pleaser!

Everything You Will Need:

3   pounds of fresh Italian sausage links
1   10 ounce jar of grape jelly
2   10 ounce bottles of chili sauce

Broil the sausages for about eight to ten minutes over medium heat, turning once only, and remove them just before they are done.

Cut the sausages into one-fourth to one-half inch bite-sized pieces.

Mix the jar of grape jelly and the two bottles of chili sauce in a two quart sauce pan and bring to a boil.

Reduce heat to low and add the sausage to the grape jelly and chili sauce mixture and let simmer for about fifteen minutes.

Serve this wonderful creation in a crockpot or other warming container and have toothpicks available for convenience.

Serves A lot! (20 For Sure.)

FRESH TOMATO & SAUSAGE SOUP

Summer, Winter, Spring or Fall, this one's good for all.

Everything You Will Need:

4	cups of chicken broth
4	cups of fresh, ripe tomatoes *(peeled, seeded and chopped)*
1	cup of celery *(finely chopped)*
1	small cauliflower *(chopped)*
½	cup of carrots *(grated)*
1½	cups of onion *(chopped)*
1	bay leaf
⅛	cup of fresh basil leaves *(chopped)*
2	teaspoons of sugar
1	teaspoon of salt
½	teaspoon of freshly ground black pepper
½	pound of fresh Italian sausage *(removed from the casings)*
1	tablespoon of olive oil
1	tablespoon of butter
8	ounces of heavy cream
	sour cream
	a few fresh basil leaves *(for garnish)*

In a large pot, combine the chicken broth, one-half of the tomatoes, one-half of the celery, all of the cauliflower, the carrot, onion, bay leaf, the chopped basil, the sugar, and the salt and pepper.

Bring to a boil.

Reduce the heat to low and simmer, covered, for twenty minutes.

Remove the bay leaf and purée the soup in a blender until completely smooth

Return the soup to the pot.

Meanwhile...
In a medium-sized skillet, cook the sausage in the olive oil over medium heat for six or seven minutes stirring occasionally with a wooden spoon to crumble the sausage.

Drain off any liquid.

Add the butter and the remaining tomatoes and celery to the sausage, and continue to cook for another six or seven minutes.

Add the sausage mixture and the cream to the soup.

Stir and heat the soup briefly for serving *(but do NOT boil!)*.

Serve with a spoon of sour cream and garnish with a basil leaf.

Serves 6 to 8 Any Time Of The Year.

PASTA E FAGIOLI WITH SAUSAGE

Serve this to a REAL Italian and watch how fast you become part of the family!

Everything You Will Need:

1	cup of small white beans
¼	cup of olive oil
1	tablespoon of butter
1½	cups of onion (*coarsely chopped*)
3	slices of lean bacon (*finely chopped*)
⅓	cup of celery (*chopped*)
½	cup of carrots (*grated*)
1	tablespoon of crushed or chopped garlic
3	tablespoons of chopped fresh basil
¼	teaspoon of dried oregano
1	pound of fresh Italian sausage (*removed from the casings*)
1	cup of fresh, ripe tomatoes (*chopped*)
1	tablespoon of fresh Italian parsley (*chopped*)
¼	teaspoon of sage
7	cups of chicken broth
1½	cups pasta (*small shells are recommended here*)
	salt
	freshly ground black pepper
	Parmesan or Romano cheese (*grated*)

Serves 6 to 8 REAL Italians.

The Day Before Serving:
Soak the beans in three to four cups of water. Let stand overnight. Drain just before using.

The Day Of Serving:
Heat the olive oil and butter in a large stock pot over medium heat.

Add the onion and bacon and cook for about six to eight minutes.

Add the celery, carrots, garlic, basil and oregano and continue to cook for about two or three minutes.

Add the Italian sausage and continue cooking all of the ingredients for about eight minutes, stirring occasionally with a wooden spoon to crumble sausage.

Add the beans, tomatoes, parsley, sage, and six cups of the chicken broth and bring the mixture to a boil.

Reduce the heat and simmer for about one and one-half hours, or until the beans are tender, stirring occasionally.

Remove two cups of the soup and purée in a blender until smooth.

Stir the purée back into the soup. Add the remaining cup of chicken broth and continue to cook, bringing the soup to a boil.

Add the pasta as well as salt and pepper to taste, and continue to cook at a slow boil for about twelve to fourteen minutes, until the pasta is tender.

Serve hot and top with grated cheese.

SICILIAN SAUSAGE SOUP

It's simply delicious!

Everything You Will Need:

I pound of fresh Italian sausage
   (removed from casings)
I½ cups of onion *(chopped)*
I tablespoon of olive oil
5 cups of chicken broth
I 28 ounce can of diced tomatoes *(in juice)*
I teaspoon of fresh basil *(chopped)*
I cup of elbow macaroni
   salt & pepper to taste

In a four to six quart stock pot, cook the sausage and the onion in the olive oil over medium heat for about ten minutes or until the onion turns transparent, stirring occasionally with a wooden spoon to crumble the sausage.

Add the chicken broth, tomatoes, the basil, and bring to a boil.

Add the macaroni, and salt and pepper to taste.

Reduce the heat to low and let the soup simmer for twenty-five minutes, partially covered, until the macaroni is tender.

Serve hot.

Serves 6 to 8 Dinner Guests.

TURKEY ITALIAN SAUSAGE SOUP WITH WILD RICE & MUSHROOMS

This is a great, hearty soup that everyone will enjoy!

Everything You Will Need:

I	pound fresh turkey Italian Sausage *(removed from casings)*
I	tablespoon of olive oil
I	tablespoon of butter
8	cups chicken broth
½	cup of fresh broccoli *(chopped)*
½	cup of leeks *(diced)*
½	cup of fresh, ripe tomatoes *(chopped)*
½	cup of fresh carrots *(chopped)*
½	cup of fresh celery *(chopped)*
I	pound of mushrooms *(chopped)*
⅔	cup of wild rice
I	teaspoon of oregano
I	tablespoon of fresh basil *(chopped)*
	salt
	freshly ground black pepper

In a large stock pot, cook the sausage in the olive oil and the butter over medium heat for ten minutes, stirring occasionally with a wooden spoon to crumble the sausage.

Add in the chicken broth, broccoli, leeks, tomatoes, carrots, celery and mushrooms, and bring to a boil.

Reduce heat to low, and let simmer for one hour.

Meanwhile...
Put the wild rice in a small pot with four cups of water and a pinch of salt, and bring to a boil.

Reduce heat to low, and let simmer for thirty minutes, uncovered.

Turn off heat, cover and let stand for another thirty minutes.

Drain the rice and add it to the soup along with the oregano, basil and salt and pepper to taste.

Cook the soup for one hour more.

Serve hot.

Warms The Bones Of 8 Who Love A Great Homemade Soup.

MEAT BALL SOUP

U gonna lova this!

Everything You Will Need:

¼ pound of fresh Italian sausage
    (removed from casings)
¼ pound of lean ground beef
I egg
½ cup of Parmesan cheese *(grated)*
4 teaspoons of crumbled bread
2 tablespoons of fresh parsley *(chopped)*
½ teaspoon of crushed or chopped garlic
7½ cups of beef broth
    salt
    freshly ground black pepper
½ pound of pasta
    (Bows or Butterflies - your choice!)

Mix the sausage, ground beef, egg, Parmesan cheese, crumbled bread, parsley, the garlic, and salt and pepper in a bowl until thoroughly blended.

Break off small pieces of the meat mixture and roll them into small, bite-sized balls (about one inch to one and one-quarter inch in diameter).

In a medium sized stock pot, bring the beef broth to a boil.

Add the meatballs and simmer for five minutes.

Add the noodles and cook for about thirteen to fifteen minutes. until the pasta is done.

Add salt and pepper to taste.

Serve hot, and top generously with more freshly grated cheese.

(This recipe makes about thirty-two small meatballs for the soup, or about eight LARGE meatballs which are great with spaghetti or for sandwiches. For the large meatballs, use the same recipe, preheat the broiler and broil for ten to twelve minutes, turning a couple of times.)

Serves 4 to Sixa u guys.

WILTED SPINACH & SAUSAGE SALAD

A wonderful salad creation! It doesn't get any better than this!

Everything You Will Need:

I	pound of fresh spinach
	(net weight, after removing the stems)
½	cup of green onion *(sliced)*
½	teaspoon of freshly ground black pepper
I	pound of fresh Italian sausage
	(removed from the casings)
5	tablespoons of olive oil
4¼	tablespoons of balsamic vinegar
2½	tablespoons of fresh lemon juice
2	teaspoons of brown sugar
½	teaspoon of salt
3	hard boiled eggs *(coarsely chopped)*
¼	cup of sun dried tomatoes *(chopped)*
	Parmesan or Romano cheese *(grated)*

Wash the spinach leaves thoroughly, and pat dry on paper towels.

Tear the leaves into bite-sized pieces and put into a large bowl.

Add the green onion and ground black pepper.

Toss the salad and chill it.

Just before serving the salad, in a medium-sized frying pan, cook the sausage in the olive oil over medium heat for twelve to fourteen minutes, stirring occasionally with a wooden spoon to crumble the sausage, being careful not to crumble the sausage too finely.

Add the vinegar, lemon juice, brown sugar, salt and sun-dried tomatoes.

Stir all of the ingredients together while simmering for another minute or two.

Slowly mix in the hot sausage dressing to the spinach.

Toss until the leaves are well coated and slightly wilted.

Add the chopped egg to the salad and toss again.

Top with the cheese.

Serve immediately while sausage is warm.

Serves 4, Perfectly.

SAUSAGE CAESAR SALAD

This is the best. Caesar would be proud of this one!

Everything You Will Need:

1	large head of Romaine lettuce
2	cups of homemade croutons
	(see recipe on page 100)
½	cup of olive oil
¼	cup of fresh lemon juice
1	teaspoon anchovy paste
1	teaspoon crushed or chopped garlic
1	tablespoon of dijon mustard
⅛	teaspoon nutmeg
½	teaspoon of worcestershire sauce
1	large egg
1	pound fresh Italian sausage links
½	cup of Parmesan or Romano cheese
	(grated)
½	teaspoon of freshly ground black pepper
	salt

Wash and tear the lettuce into pieces.

Put the lettuce into a colander lined with paper towels, and place the colander in the refrigerator.

Make the homemade croutons. *(see recipe on page 100)*.

To Make The Dressing:
Whisk the olive oil, lemon juice, anchovy paste, minced garlic, dijon mustard, nutmeg and worcestershire sauce in a small bowl until it is well blended.

Bring about one quart of water to a boil in a small pan.

Gently place the egg in the boiling water with tongs, and continue to boil over high heat for one minute only.

Remove the egg and cool under cold running water.

Carefully break the egg and add the yolk only to the dressing.

Whisk the egg into the dressing until smooth, and set the dressing aside in the refrigerator.

To Make The Salad:
Broil the sausage for fifteen to eighteen minutes, turing occasionally, until done.

Cut the sausage diagonally into one-fourth to one-half inch, bite-sized pieces.

In a large salad bowl, combine the lettuce, enough dressing to coat the lettuce well, and black pepper.

Serves 4. (With Compliments To The Chef!)

Mix together well.

Saving a little for later, add the cheese and toss the salad again.

Add the sausage and croutons and toss the salad again.

Top off the salad with fresh ground pepper and the remaining cheese.

Serve immediately while sausage is warm.

FRENCH QUARTER PASTA SALAD

Put a bowl of this in your next buffet line and watch how fast it disappears!

Everything You Will Need:

1	pound of pasta *(Use Rotelle on this one)*
1½	cups of New Orleans style olive salad *(see recipe on page 101)*
4	ounces of salami *(julienned)*
4	ounces of Provolone cheese *(cubed)*
3	hard boiled eggs *(chopped)*
2	tablespoons of red wine vinegar
1	pound of fresh Italian sausage links

Cook the pasta according to directions on the package.

Drain in a colander and rinse with cool water.

In a large bowl, mix the pasta and the olive salad together until the pasta is well coated.

Mix in the salami, cheese, eggs and red wine vinegar.

Set aside and refrigerate.

Broil the sausage for fifteen to eighteen minutes, turning occasionally, until done.

Cut the sausages into one-fourth to one-half inch, bite-sized pieces.

Mix the hot sausage into the pasta salad.

Serve immediately while the sausage is still warm.

Serves 8. Be Sure To Make Enough!

TUSCAN FOYA BREAD & SAUSAGE SALAD

Originally a peasant dish, this salad now finds a worthy place on any table, and it's good "fo-ya".

Everything You Will Need:

6	tablespoons of olive oil
3	tablespoons of red wine vinegar
I	tablespoon of lemon juice
½	teaspoon of black pepper
I	tablespoon of butter
6	ounces of fresh Italian or French bread *(a nice crusty roll, cut in half)*
½	pound of fresh Italian sausage links
8	ounces of premixed salad greens
½	cup of fresh Roma tomatoes *(chopped)*
10	large, fresh basil leaves *(torn into pieces)*
4	ounces of fresh Mozzarella cheese *(diced into one-half inch cubes or coarsely grated)*

To Make The Dressing:
Whisk the olive oil, red wine vinegar, lemon juice, and pepper in a small bowl.

To Make The Salad:
Preheat the broiler.

Broil the sausage for fifteen to eighteen minutes, turning occasionally, until done.

Butter the bread slices and put them in the broiler with the sausage, but only for a minute or so, until the butter is melted.

Remove the bread from the broiler, and tear into bite-sized pieces.

Put the bread into a large salad bowl with one-half of the dressing, and toss well.

When the sausage is finished cooking, cut into one-quarter to one-half inch, bite-sized pieces.

Add the greens, tomatoes and basil to the bread and toss well.

Pour in the remaining dressing and toss again.

Add the sausage and cheese.

Serve immediately while the sausage is warm.

Serves 4 As A Salad Course.

SAUSAGE SINATRA

This dish, originally known as "Steak Sinatra", was the creation of a restaurant in Palm Springs, California. As its popularity grew, it was adapted by other restaurants from California to Alaska using sausage. This is California cuisine at its best!

Everything You Will Need:

1   pound of fresh Italian sausage links
2   tablespoons of olive oil
½   medium green (bell) pepper
     (sliced lengthwise)
½   medium red bell pepper *(sliced lengthwise)*
1   medium onion *(sliced)*
6   ounces of fresh mushrooms *(sliced)*
¼   cup of red wine
     salt
     freshly ground black pepper

In a large skillet, cook the sausages in one-half of the olive oil for five minutes over medium-high heat, turning once only.

Mix in the bell peppers, onion and the rest of the olive oil.

Continue to cook for about another five minutes, stirring a couple of times.

Reduce the heat to low, cover, and let it simmer for five minutes more.

Mix in the mushrooms and red wine.

Cover, raise the heat to medium-high, and cook for ten minutes.

Still covered, increase the heat to high for another minute or two.

Place a sausage on a plate and serve with the bell pepper, onion and mushrooms.

Add salt and pepper to taste and serve hot.

(Delicious with Saffron rice or Creamy Smooth Polenta. See recipes on page 102 and 103.)

Serves 4 Strangers In The Night.

SICILIAN MEAT ROLL

"Braciole" in Italian.

Everything You Will Need:

¼   cup of Parmesan or Romano cheese
(grated)
⅛   teaspoon of nutmeg
¼   teaspoon of salt
½   teaspoon of freshly ground black pepper
⅓   cup of fresh parsley *(chopped)*
1   fresh egg
½   pound of fresh Italian sausage
(removed from the casings)
1   1½ to 2 pound thin flank steak
(as wide as possible)
4   thin slices of Black Forest ham
1   small carrot *(sliced in fourths, lengthwise)*
1   celery stalk *(sliced in half, lengthwise)*
2   slices of Provolone cheese
2   eggs *(hard boiled & sliced in fourths)*
¼   cup of olive oil
2   medium onions *(sliced)*
¾   cup of red wine
kitchen string

Serves 6.

In a large bowl, combine the Parmesan or Romano cheese, nutmeg, salt, pepper, parsley, egg and sausage. Mix well by hand.

Pound out the flank steak to a nice rectangular shape.

Spread the sausage mixture over the steak, out to about an inch from the edges.

Lay the ham slices over the sausage mixture.

Lay the carrot lengthwise across the filling, on top of the ham, then lay the celery along side the carrot in the same manner.

Roll the slices of Provolone cheese, and place the rolls end to end along side the carrot.

Lay the egg slices over the center length of the meat roll.

Tightly roll up the meat and tie it together in five or six places. *(Tip: Cut about six pieces of string, fourteen to fifteen inches long, then lay them out. Set the meat roll over them. It helps to have an assistant put a finger on the knot!)*

Wipe the entire roll with about one-half of the olive oil.

Sprinkle the roll with the salt and pepper.

Wipe the bottom of a shallow nine by thirteen inch glass baking dish with the remaining olive oil.

Put the onion slices in the dish.

Place the meat roll on a rack in the dish.

Pour the wine over the meat roll.

Preheat the oven to 350 degrees.

Roast the meat roll for one and one-half hours, basting occasionally with olive oil and its own juices.

When the meat roll is done cooking, remove the string and let stand for only a couple of minutes.

Slice the roll into one inch pieces.

Serve with a spoonful of the onions and a side of Orange Salad *(found on page 100)*.

SAVORY SOUTHWESTERN SAUSAGE

Serve this to the family once, and it'll become a regular favorite!

Everything You Will Need:

1	pound of fresh turkey or chicken Italian sausage links
1	tablespoon of butter
1	cup of chicken broth
1	cup of fresh, ripe tomatoes *(peeled, seeded, & chopped)*
4	green onions *(chopped)*
½	cup of fresh cilantro *(chopped)*
1¼	tablespoons of fresh lime juice
6	burrito sized flour tortillas
2½	ounces of Monterey jack cheese *(grated)*
2½	ounces of cheddar cheese *(grated)* *(Mix the Monterey jack and cheddar cheeses together in a bowl.)*

sliced avocado, sour cream, fresh salsa and lime wedges for garnish

In a large frying pan, cook the sausage in the butter over medium heat for eight to ten minutes, turning a couple of times.

Add the chicken broth.

Sprinkle on the tomatoes, green onion and cilantro.

Raise the heat to medium-high.

Cover and let it simmer for ten minutes.

Stir in the lime juice.

Cover again and continue to simmer for another three to five minutes.

Have the tortillas warmed and ready.

Place a sausage in a tortilla.

Spoon on some of the mixture and sprinkle on some of the grated cheese.

Fold in three sides of the tortilla, bottom first, to hold in the juices, much like a burrito and serve.

(Serve this dish with sliced avocado, sour cream, fresh salsa, and a couple of lime wedges.)

Serves 4 to 6.

STUFFED PEPPERS

....Just like Mom used to make...

Everything You Will Need:

1	cup of uncooked white rice
1	pound of fresh Italian sausage
	(removed from the casings)
1	tablespoon of olive oil
1 ½	cup of onion *(chopped)*
1	teaspoon of garlic salt
1 ½	cups of fresh, ripe tomatoes *(chopped)*
½	cup of Parmesan or Romano cheese
1	cup of Mozzarella cheese *(grated)*
1	15 ounce can of tomato sauce
4	green (bell) peppers

Cook the rice according to the directions on the package and set aside.

In a medium-sized frying pan cook the sausage in the olive oil, onion and garlic salt over medium-high heat for eight to ten minutes, stirring with a wooden spoon to crumble the sausage.

Add the sausage and onion to the rice along with the tomatoes, Parmesan or Romano cheese, Mozzarella cheese and one cup of the tomato sauce.

Mix all of the ingredients together.

Fill the peppers with the rice mixture and place in a baking dish.

Spoon the remaining tomato sauce over the tops of the peppers.

Preheat oven to 350 degrees.

Bake at 350 degrees for forty-five minutes.

Serve hot.

Serves 4.

ITALIAN SAUSAGE KEBAB

Serve this fare over a bed of Rice Pilaf with a small salad and garlic bread for a terrific meal anytime!

Everything You Will Need:

1	pound fresh Italian sausage links *(cut into thirds)*
1	large onion *(cut into wedges)*
1	red (bell) pepper *(cut into eighths)*
1	green (bell) pepper *(cut into eighths)*
2	fresh, ripe tomatoes *(cut into eighths)*
½	pound fresh mushrooms *(whole)*
¼	cup of olive oil
1	tablespoon of red wine vinegar

Carefully slide the cut food pieces onto metal skewers, alternating the sausage and the various vegetables.

Mix the olive oil and red wine vinegar together for basting.

Barbecue or broil the kebabs for about sixteen to eighteen minutes, basting and turning occasionally.

Serve over a bed of rice pilaf.

(Rice Pilaf may possibly have been invented to go along with this dish. See how it's made on page 102. The Mardi Gras Small Dinner Salad found on page 101 is also delicious with this).

Serves 4.

CONCHIPACHO

a.k.a. Cowboy Beans & Sausage Over Perfect White Rice

Everything You Will Need:

1	cup of dried black beans
2	tablespoons of butter
1½	cups of onion *(chopped)*
¼	cup of green onion *(chopped)*
1	teaspoon of crushed or chopped garlic
¼	teaspoon of salt
½	teaspoon of freshly ground black pepper
1	teaspoon of dried oregano
5½	cups of water
1½	cups of chicken broth
½	teaspoon of rubbed sage
1	pound of fresh Italian sausage *(removed from the casings)*
1	tablespoon of olive oil
1	portion of perfect white rice *(see recipe on page 102)*

Serves 4 To 6, At Home Or On The Range.

A Day Before Serving:
Soak the beans in enough water to cover them by a couple of inches or so, cover and let stand overnight.

The Day Of Serving:
In a medium-sized pot, melt the butter.

Add the onion, green onions, the garlic, and cook for six to eight minutes over medium heat.

Drain the water from the beans and rinse them in cold water.

Add the beans, salt, black pepper, oregano, sage, the water, and the chicken broth. Bring the mixture to a boil.

Reduce the heat to low, and simmer, uncovered, for two hours, stirring occasionally.

When the beans have been simmering for about one hour and fifteen minutes, cook the sausage in the olive oil in a small skillet for about ten to twelve minutes, stirring occasionally with a wooden spoon to crumble the sausage.

When the beans have been cooking for one and one-half hours, add in the sausage and continue to simmer for another one-half hour.

Meanwhile...
Prepare the white rice according to the recipe.

Place each serving of rice in a deep dish.

Top the rice with a ladle of conchipacho and sausage and serve hot.

FRESH SPINACH & SAUSAGE PIES

Olive Oyl used to make these for Popeye!

Everything You Will Need:

¾   pound of fresh spinach leaves
      (net weight, after removing the stems)
¼   cup of salt
3   tablespoons of olive oil
¾   pound of fresh Italian sausage
      (removed from the casings)
3   fresh basil leaves *(torn into pieces)*
¾   cup of Parmesan or Romano cheese *(grated)*
¼   teaspoon of freshly ground black pepper
2   packages of ready-to-use pie crusts for a
      nine inch pie. *(four 11 inch rounds)*
2   fresh egg yolks
1   teaspoon of milk

Makes 16 pies.

Wash the spinach leaves thoroughly.

Tear the leaves into pieces and put into a large colander.

Generously sprinkle the spinach leaves with salt.

Toss the leaves well, put them into a large bowl and let stand for at least one hour, unrefrigerated.

Rinse and wring out the water in the spinach leaves by hand. *(Don't be afraid...wring them out like a towel.)*

Spread the leaves out and pat dry on paper towels.

Dry out the large bowl and pour in the olive oil.

Crumble in the sausage.

Add the spinach leaves, basil, cheese, black pepper., then mix thoroughly by hand.

Cut the pie crusts into fourths and put a portion of the filling on each piece.

Fold over and crimp the edges of the two sides with a fork.

Poke small holes or slit the top of each pie to let the heat escape.

Beat the egg yolks and milk, and brush the top of each pie.

Preheat the oven to 350 degrees.

Place the pies on a cookie sheet and bake for thirty to thirty-five minutes.

Serve hot.

Hoppin' John & Hot Sausage

Here's my smokin' version of this celebrated southern dish.

Everything You Will Need:

1	cup of dried black-eyed peas
3	tablespoons of butter
3	slices of bacon *(chopped)*
1	teaspoon of crushed or chopped garlic
1½	cups of onion *(chopped)*
½	cup of green onion *(chopped)*
3	cups of chicken broth
¼	teaspoon of salt
½	teaspoon of freshly ground black pepper
½	teaspoon of crushed red pepper
¼	teaspoon of rubbed sage
¼	teaspoon of liquid smoke
½	pound of smoked ham hock
1	pound of fresh hot Italian sausage links
1	cup of white rice
3	cups of water
½	teaspoon of tabasco sauce

Serves 4 to 6 One Heck Of A Meal!

A Day Before Serving:
Soak the peas in enough water to cover them by a couple of inches or so. Cover and let stand overnight.

The Day Of Serving:
Heat one-half of the butter in a six quart stock pot over medium heat.

Add the bacon, garlic, onion, and green onion, and cook for eight to ten minutes over medium heat, stirring occasionally.

Drain the water from the black eyed peas and rinse them off with cold water.

Add the peas to the pot along with the chicken broth, three cups of water, salt, black pepper, crushed red pepper, sage, liquid smoke, and ham hock.

Bring to a boil, stirring occasionally. Reduce the heat to low and simmer for one and one-half hours.

About one hour and ten minutes into simmering the mixture, broil the sausage for fifteen to sixteen minutes, turning a couple of times.

Cut the sausage into one-fourth to one-half inch, bite-sized pieces.

When the mixture has simmered for one and one-half hours, stir in the rice, the remaining butter, and the broiled sausage.

Cover and continue to simmer for another thirty to thirty-five minutes, until the rice is tender. *(It may be necessary to add a little water to finish the rice.)*

Stir in the tabasco sauce and serve in a chili bowl.

STUFFED EGGPLANT

Tempt a vegetarian with this one!

Everything You Will Need:

1   eggplant *(1 to 1¼ pounds)*
      salt
1   cup of onion *(chopped)*
3   tablespoons of olive oil
2   tablespoons of crushed or chopped garlic
½   pound of fresh Italian sausage
      (removed from the casings)
½   pound of lean ground beef
2   cups of fresh, ripe tomatoes
      (peeled, seeded & chopped)
2   tablespoons of fresh basil *(chopped)*
2   tablespoons of fresh parsley *(chopped)*
¼   cup of Italian seasoned bread crumbs
      freshly ground black pepper
¼   cup Mozzarella cheese *(grated)*

Serves 4 Fallen Vegetarians Shamelessly.

Wash the eggplant, and cut it in half lengthwise.

With a spoon, carve out part of the interior of each half while removing seeds, leaving a neat cavity for the filling.

Rinse the eggplant shell with water.

Sprinkle the insides of the eggplant halves with salt, turn them upside down, and let them stand for about one hour on a rack (to allow for breathing).

In a medium-sized frying pan cook the onion and garlic in the olive oil over medium-high heat for about three minutes.

Add the sausage and ground beef.

Cook for about four to five minutes more, stirring occasionally with a wooden spoon to mix the meat.

Mix in the tomatoes, basil and parsley.

Cook for two or three more minutes.

Turn off the heat, and when cool enough to handle, thoroughly mix in the breadcrumbs and salt and pepper to taste.

Preheat the oven to 350 degrees.

Fill the eggplant halves with the filling, and put them in a shallow glass baking dish. *(It may be necessary to touch the sides of the halves together to keep them propped up and level)*.

Add about one-half inch of water into baking dish.

Bake the halves for forty-five minutes at 350 degrees.

Carefully pull out the oven rack and sprinkle on the Mozzarella cheese.

Bake for about another ten minutes, or until the cheese has melted.

Remove the eggplant halves from the pan, and serve hot.

(As an alternative, zucchini (small Italian squashes) may be used. They will require the same treatment and cooking time, however the mixture listed here will fill about eight zucchini).

Italian Sausage & Potatoes

A great lunchtime or dinner meal; simple to make, and great tasting too!

Everything You Will Need:

I	pound fresh Italian sausage links
¼	cup of olive oil
2	potatoes *(peeled & sliced thinly into rounds)*
I	large onion *(sliced)*
2	green (bell) peppers *(seeded & sliced)*
I	teaspoon dried oregano
I	teaspoon dried basil
I	teaspoon of crushed or chopped garlic
	salt and freshly ground black pepper

Broil the sausage for about six to eight minutes, turning once only.

Cut the sausage into one-fourth to one-half inch bite-sized pieces.

Cover the bottom of a large electric skillet or frying pan with the olive oil.

Fry the potatoes for about ten to twelve minutes over medium-high heat, turning frequently with a spatula.

Add the sausage, onion, bell pepper, oregano, basil, garlic, and salt and pepper to taste, to the potatoes.

Cook over medium heat, covered, for almost twenty minutes or until the potatoes are tender, turning occasionally.

Serve hot.

A wonderful compliment to this dish is the Tomato And Onion Salad found on page 100.

A Hearty Dinner For 4 To 6 persons.

SAUSAGE & SHRIMP IN SAFFRON ORZO

Fasten your seatbelts! This is a "hands-on" recipe from start to finish. Don't even THINK about trying this one without an assistant! An unforgettable meal well worth the effort!

Everything You Will Need:

I	pound of fresh Italian sausage link
⅓	cup of olive oil
4	tablespoons of butter
¾	pound of fresh medium-sized shrimp *(de-veined & cleaned)*
I	tablespoon of fresh basil *(chopped)*
½	teaspoon of dried oregano
¼	teaspoon of crushed red pepper
¼	cup of dry vermouth
4	teaspoons of crushed or chopped garlic
4	fresh, ripe Roma tomatoes *(peeled, seeded & chopped)*
I¾	cups of chicken broth
I½	cups of onion *(chopped)*
I	cup of orzo pasta
¼	teaspoon of saffron
⅓	cup of white wine
I	cup of water
½	cup of Parmesan or Romano cheese *(grated)*
	salt and freshly ground pepper

Serves 4 Of Your Most Appreciative Gourmet Dish Fans.

In a large frying pan, cook the sausage in one and one-half tablespoons of the olive oil and one and one-half tablespoons of the butter over medium-high heat for about twelve to fourteen minutes, turning occasionally.

Remove the sausages before they are fully cooked.

Cut the sausages into one-fourth to one-half inch, bite-sized pieces and set aside in a small bowl.

Raise the heat to high.

Put the shrimp into the skillet.

Stir the shrimp to coat them in the butter and oil.

Add the basil, oregano, crushed red pepper, the vermouth, and one-half of the garlic.

Sauté the shrimp over high heat for about three minutes.

Remove the shrimp only and set them aside in a small bowl.

Put the tomatoes and one-third cup of the chicken broth into the skillet and let boil for about three minutes.

Add the sausage back in. Turn off the heat and stir well.

Meanwhile, back at the range...
Heat the remaining olive oil in a ten inch, non-stick skillet.

Add the onion and remaining garlic, and cook them over medium-high heat for three or four minutes.

Add in the pasta and the saffron.

Stir well, until the pasta is well coated.

Pour in the white wine and let simmer for about five minutes.

Separately, dilute the remaining chicken broth with the cup of water.

Stir in three-fourths of a cup of the diluted chicken broth to the mixture and let simmer until the liquid is mostly absorbed (about five minutes), stirring frequently.

Return to the first pan with the sausage. Turn the heat on to medium-high.

Add the pasta in with the sausage and another three-fourths cup of the diluted broth.

Continue to simmer the mixture and stir until the liquid is absorbed again.

Stir in the remaining diluted broth and continue simmering for a final six to eight minutes.

Just before the liquid is absorbed, add in the shrimp and the remaining butter.

Continue to simmer for a couple more minutes. When the liquid is absorbed and the pasta is tender, turn off the heat and stir in the cheese until the sauce is creamy smooth.

Add salt and pepper to taste.

Serve hot.

ROASTED TURKEY & SAUSAGE ROLL

We're talkin' turkey here...this one melts in your mouth!

Everything You Will Need:

I	5 pound boneless turkey breast
	(in one piece, with skin)
½	teaspoon of dried oregano
¼	teaspoon of salt
½	teaspoon of freshly ground black pepper
¾	cup of butter
	(let temper for about 15 minutes before using)
½	pound of fresh Italian sausage
	(removed from the casings)
¼	cup of olive oil
	ground pepper medley
	garlic salt
	kitchen string

Serves 6. (Maybe 8!)

Neatly bone (or have your butcher do it) a turkey breast (in one piece) to net about five pounds.

Remove and save the skin in one large piece.

Lay the breast out and pound it to an even thickness, pushing the sides to form a rectangular piece. Lay the breast on it's back side with the cut side up.

Spread the butter over the breast, then sprinkle on the oregano, salt, and black pepper.

Crumble on the Italian sausage.

Neatly and tightly roll the breast, cover it with the skin, and tie it together in five or six places. *(Tip: Cut about six pieces of string fourteen to fifteen inches long, and lay them out. Set the turkey roll over them. It helps to have an assistant put a finger on the knot, but really, it's not as difficult as it might sound!)*

Rub the roll thoroughly with the olive oil. Sprinkle on the pepper medley and garlic salt to taste.

Place the turkey roll on a roast rack and put into a nine by thirteen inch glass baking dish.

Preheat the oven to 350 degrees. Roast for about one and one-half hour, brushing or basting occasionally with its own juices.

When the turkey roll is finished roasting, test it with a roast-meat thermometer which, in the center the breast, should read 168 to 170 degrees.

Let the roasted turkey roll stand for just a couple of minutes before carving.

Cut into one inch slices and serve hot.

LASAGNE ROLLS

This will probably be the best tasting lasagne you'll ever have. Enjoy!

Everything You Will Need:

½   pound of lasagne noodles
I   pound of fresh Italian sausage
        (removed from the casings)
2   tablespoons of butter
I5   ounces of Ricotta cheese
I   cup of Parmesan cheese *(grated)*
¼   teaspoon of nutmeg
        salt
¼   teaspoon of black pepper
3¼   cups of Caryn's Special Sunday Sauce
        (see recipe on page 98)
2¼   cups of Mornay Sauce *(see recipe on page 103)*

Prepare the lasagne noodles according to the directions on the package.

In a medium-sized frying pan, cook the sausage in the butter over medium heat for about ten minutes, stirring occasionally with a wooden spoon to crumble the sausage.

Remove the sausage from the heat, drain off any liquid, and let cool for a couple of minutes.

In a bowl, mix the sausage with the Ricotta cheese, Parmesan cheese, nutmeg, and salt and pepper.

Baste the bottom of a nine by thirteen inch glass baking dish with one-half cup of Caryn's Special Sunday sauce.

Spread a thin layer of the filling on the noodles.

Roll the noodles and place them in the dish, seam side down.

Pour the Mornay sauce evenly over the top of the lasagne rolls.

Pour two cups of Caryn's Special Sunday sauce evenly over the top of lasagne rolls.

Preheat the oven to 350 degrees.

Bake the rolls for forty minutes.

Serve hot with the remaining sauce on the side.

Serves 6 to 8 Lucky Diners.

PAPA'S PENNE PASTA PUTTANESCA

This fare was made famous in Italy, being served up by "ladies of the night" to their patrons! Here's my spiced up version using hot Italian sausage!

Everything You Will Need:

1	pound of fresh hot Italian sausage links
¼	cup of olive oil
2	tablespoons of butter
1	tablespoon of crushed or chopped garlic
1½	cups of onion *(chopped)*
2	cups of fresh, ripe tomatoes *(peeled, seeded & chopped)*
¼	teaspoon of crushed red pepper
3	tablespoons of fresh basil *(chopped)*
1	cup black olives *(pitted & sliced)*
2½	tablespoons of capers
1	pound of pasta *(Penne, of course!)*
	salt and freshly ground black pepper
	Parmesan or Romano cheese *(grated)*

Services 4.

Broil the sausage for about eight to ten minutes, turning once only.

Remove sausages from broiler, and cut them into one-quarter to one-half inch, bite-sized pieces.

(To make sure your sauce and pasta are timed correctly, bring a pot of water to a boil now, and about fifteen minutes before finishing this recipe, cook the pasta according to the directions on the package.)

In a large frying pan, heat the olive oil, butter, and garlic.

When the butter has melted, add the onion, and cook for about ten minutes over medium heat.

Add in the sausage, tomatoes, the red pepper, and simmer for five minutes, stirring occasionally.

Add the basil, and continue to simmer for five minutes more.

Add in the black olives and capers.

Reduce heat to low and let simmer for about another five minutes, or until the pasta is ready.

Drain the pasta in a colander and return back to the pot.

Add the sauce and gently mix together until the pasta is well coated.

Add salt and pepper to taste.

Serve hot and top with cheese.

SAUSAGE & ONION ALFREDO

Inspired by a recipe from the famous Roman restaurant, Alfredo's. Serve this one for a special occasion!

Everything You Will Need:

I	pound of fresh Italian sausage links
I	large onion *(finely sliced)*
¼	cup of butter
⅔	cup of white wine *(chardonnay)*
I ½	cups of heavy cream
¼	teaspoon of nutmeg
I	pound of pasta *(Radiatore is the one here)*
⅔	cup of freshly grated Parmesan or Romano cheese
	salt & pepper

Serves 4.

Broil the sausage for eight to ten minutes, turning once only.

Remove the sausages from the broiler and cut into one-fourth to one-half inch, bite-sized pieces and set aside.

(To make sure your sauce and pasta are timed correctly, bring a pot of water to a boil now. Cook the pasta according to the directions on the package.)

Meanwhile...
In a large frying pan or electric skillet, cook the onion in the butter over medium to medium-low heat for fifteen minutes, being careful not to burn the butter.

Add in the sausage and the wine.

Raise the heat to medium-high and let simmer for eight to ten minutes, stirring occasionally with a wooden spoon.

Reduce the heat to low.

Stir in the cream and the nutmeg and let simmer, stirring occasionally, for ten more minutes, or until pasta is ready.

Drain the pasta in a colander and return back to the pot.

Add the sauce and the grated cheese. Gently mix together until the pasta is well coated.

Add salt and pepper to taste.

Serve hot.

FRESH TOMATO & CARROT SAUCE

A pasta dish you can't refuse!

Everything You Will Need:

1	tablespoon of butter
1	tablespoon of olive oil
1	pound of fresh Italian sausage
	(removed from the casings)
1¼	cups of onion *(finely chopped)*
1	teaspoon of crushed or chopped garlic
1	cup of white wine
2	cups of fresh, ripe tomatoes
	(peeled, seeded & chopped)
½	cup of chicken broth
1	cup of carrots *(coarsely grated)*
⅓	cup of fresh parsley *(chopped)*
1	pound pasta
	(Rotelle or Gemelli for this one)
	salt and freshly ground black pepper
	Parmesan or Romano cheese *(grated)*

Serves 4 to 6. (Don't expect any leftovers!)

Heat the butter and the olive oil in a large frying pan.

Add the sausage, onion, and garlic.

(To make sure your sauce and pasta are timed correctly, begin to bring a pot of water to a boil now. Cook the pasta according to the directions on the package.)

Meanwhile...
Cook the sausage, onion and garlic over medium heat for five or six minutes, stirring occasionally with a wooden spoon to crumble the sausage.

Add the wine.

Raise the heat and simmer for five or six more minutes.

Add the tomatoes and chicken broth.

Continue to cook for six or seven more minutes over medium-high heat.

Add the carrots and parsley.

Cook for five or six minutes more, or until the carrots are tender.

Drain the pasta in a colander and return back to the pot.

Add the sauce and gently mix together until the pasta is well coated.

Add salt and pepper to taste.

Serve hot and top with grated cheese.

OUR OWN CLASSIC BOLOGNESE MEAT SAUCE

Boy Oh Boy! A really thick and rich meat sauce that will win over anyone!

Everything You Will Need:

2½   tablespoons of virgin olive oil
6   tablespoons of butter
4   teaspoons of crushed or chopped garlic
1¾   cups of onion *(finely chopped)*
½   cup of carrots *(finely chopped)*
⅓   cup of celery *(finely chopped)*
4   ounces of bacon *(chopped)*
¾   pound of fresh Italian sausage
     (removed from the casings)
½   pound of lean beefsteak *(finely chopped)*
½   cup Marsala wine
1   tablespoon of fresh basil *(chopped)*
½   tablespoon of dried oregano
⅛   teaspoon of fresh nutmeg
     salt and freshly ground black pepper
1   teaspoon of sugar
1   28 ounce can of peeled and diced tomatoes
     (in juice)
2   tablespoons of tomato paste
¼   pound of mushrooms *(sliced)*
½   cup of fresh parsley *(chopped)*
1   pound of pasta
     (Mostacciolli or Rigatoni goes great
     with this sauce)
     Parmesan or Romano cheese *(grated)*

4 To 6 Delighted Guests Will Thank You.

Heat the olive oil and one-half of the butter in a large frying pan.

Add the garlic, onion, carrot, celery and bacon.

Cook over low heat for about four or five minutes or until the vegetables are tender.

Add the sausage meat and chopped beef.

Raise the heat and sauté for eight to ten minutes or until the meat just begins to brown, stirring occasionally with a wooden spoon to crumble the meat.

Add the Marsala wine and stir in the basil, oregano, the nutmeg. Season to taste with salt and ground pepper.

Mix in the sugar, the tomatoes in their juice and the tomato paste.

Reduce the heat to low, stir thoroughly, and let simmer for thirty minutes, uncovered.

Separately, sauté the mushrooms for two to three minutes in the remaining butter along with the parsley.

Mix the sautéd mushrooms into the sauce. Reduce the heat enough to keep warm until serving.

Cook the pasta according to the directions on the package.

Drain the pasta in a colander and return back to the pot.

Add the sauce and gently mix together. Add salt and pepper to taste. Place in a warm serving dish, serve hot, and top with cheese.

CREAMY PASTA WITH EGGS, SAUSAGE & LEEKS

A fabulous dish with a subtle touch of style.

Everything You Will Need:

I	pound of pasta *(Gemelli or Fusilli go well with this)*
4	cups of leeks *(cleaned and thinly sliced)*
I	pound of fresh Italian sausage *(removed from the casings)*
6	tablespoons of butter
4	eggs
¼	cup of heavy cream
I	cup of fresh Parmesan or Romano cheese *(grated)*
	salt and pepper
¼	cup of fresh parsley *(chopped)*

Cook the pasta according to the directions on the package, drain thoroughly in a colander, and set aside.

In a large frying pan, cook the sausage in one-half of the butter over medium heat for about five or six minutes, stirring occasionally with a wooden spoon to crumble the sausage being careful to not crumble the sausage too finely.

Raise the heat to medium-high.

Add the leeks and the remaining butter. Continue to cook for another five minutes.

Beat the eggs, cream, and one-half cup of the grated cheese in a small bowl and set aside.

Add the pasta to the sausage and leeks.

Add in the eggs, cream and cheese.

Raise the heat to high and stir the mixture constantly for a couple of minutes until the eggs are done.

Add the parsley, and salt and pepper to taste.

Give the mix another stir.

Top with the remaining grated cheese.

Serve hot.

Serves 4 To 6.

CARYN'S SPECIAL SUNDAY SAUCE

This is one of Papa's favorites. It takes a couple of hours to cook and fills the house with great aroma!

Everything You Will Need:

2	28 ounce cans of peeled and diced tomatoes in juice
1	28 ounce can of tomato puree
1	12 ounce can of tomato paste
2	cups of water
1	cup of chopped parsley
2	cloves of crushed or chopped garlic
2	teaspoons of salt
1½	teaspoons of dried oregano
¼	cup of fresh basil *(chopped)*
1	teaspoon of fresh ground pepper
3	cups of onion *(chopped)*
8	ounces of sliced fresh mushrooms
3	tablespoons of sugar
1	pound of fresh Italian sausage links
1	pound of chicken thighs *(skin on)*
1	pound of pasta
	(your call...Spaghetti, Cappellini, Angel Hair, Linguini, Mostaccioli, Rigatoni ...they're all great with this sauce!)
	Parmesan or Romano cheese *(grated)*

Serves 4 To 6 Family & Friends.

Put all of the ingredients except for the sausage and chicken into a large stock pot and mix together well.

Bring to a slow boil over medium-high heat.

Reduce the heat to low.

Add the sausage links and the chicken thighs.

Simmer the sauce, uncovered, for almost two and one-half hours, stirring occasionally.

(Warning: You'll be tempted whenever you pass by the kitchen, but keep your fingers off the sausages! Admittedly though, Papa always sneaks a sausage as a quick snack after they've cooked about two hours in the sauce! You may want to keep a piece of Italian bread next to the pot!)

(Cook the pasta so that it is ready about the same time as the sauce is finished.)

Remove the chicken and sausage, and place them in a separate serving dish.

Drain the pasta in a colander and return back to the pot.

Add one cup of the sauce to the cooked pasta, and gently mix together until the pasta is well coated.

Serve the pasta and ladle a spoonful of sauce over each plate.

Top with a sausage and the grated cheese.

Serve hot with the chicken on the side.

(This makes three quarts of sauce and it freezes very well, so put some aside in the refrigerator for the next day, and some in the freezer for other recipes calling for sauce.)

TOMATO & ONION SALAD

Everything You Will Need To Serve 4 To 6:

10	fresh, ripe Roma tomatoes *(sliced into eighths)*
½	cup of red onion *(thinly sliced)*
2	tablespoons of fresh basil *(chopped)*
½	cup of olive oil
2½	tablespoons of red wine vinegar
½	teaspoon of dried oregano
¼	teaspoon of salt
½	teaspoon of freshly ground pepper

Combine all of the ingredients in a bowl and mix together well.

Refrigerate the mixture for about an hour or so, giving it an occasionally stir.

(A good complimentary side dish is important. This one is terrific with **Italian Sausage And Potatoes***, found on page 80.)*

ORANGE SALAD

Everything You Will Need To Serve 4:

I	teaspoon of ground anise or anise seed
4	good-looking oranges *(nicely peeled & sliced)*
3	tablespoons of olive oil
I	tablespoon of fresh lemon juice
¼	teaspoon of freshly ground black pepper

In a small bowl, sprinkle the anise over the orange slices.

Mix the orange slices and the anise well, and put the bowl into the refrigerator until chilled.

Just before serving, whisk the olive oil, lemon juice and black pepper together well and pour over the chilled oranges.

(The **Sicilian Meat Roll***, found on page 64 is great, but serve a side of this with it, and it'll really put your guests over the edge!)*

HOMEMADE CROUTONS

Everything You Will Need:

3	tablespoons of butter
I½	tablespoons of olive oil
I	teaspoon of crushed or chopped garlic
2	cups of French or Italian bread *(cut into bite-sized pieces of about one-half inch squares)*

Heat the butter, olive oil and garlic in a medium-sized frying pan.

Raise the heat to medium-high.

Add the breadcrumbs.

Cook the breadcrumbs for about five minutes, stirring as needed, until they are well toasted on all sides. *(Be careful not to burn them).*

(You can't beat "homemade" anything! Use this in the **Sausage Caesar Salad** *found on page 56.)*

MARDI GRAS SMALL DINNER SALAD

Everything You Will Need For A Single Serving:

I   serving of mixed greens
    (*mixed baby European greens work great!*)
1½ tablespoons of New Orleans Style Olive
    Salad (*see recipe to your right*)
½   teaspoon of red wine vinegar
I   piece of Hearts of Palm (*per serving*)
    (*cut into rounds*)
    crumbled Feta cheese

Wash the greens.

Add the olive salad and red wine vinegar to the greens.

Toss the salad well and top off with the Hearts of Palm and Feta cheese.

Refrigerate for ten minutes, if desired, and serve chilled.

(*This is a great small salad to accompany any meal.*)

NEW ORLEANS STYLE OLIVE SALAD

Everything You Will Need To Make 3fi Cups:

¼   cup of Italian style olives (*pitted*)
1¼ cups of green olives (*pitted*)
1½ cups of black olives (*pitted*)
½   cup of pimento (*chopped*)
2½ tablespoons of capers
⅔   cup of fresh parsley (*finely chopped*)
2   teaspoons of oregano
½   teaspoon of freshly ground black pepper
1¼ cups of olive oil
2   teaspoons of crushed or chopped garlic

Coarsely chop the olives.

Put the olives, pimento, capers, parsley, oregano, black pepper, and garlic in a large bowl and mix thoroughly.

Place the olive salad into a one quart glass Mason jar.

Add the olive oil.

Put the lid on the jar and let stand over night.

(*This is the key ingredient to the* **New Orleans Style Muffaletta Sandwich** *found on page 32, the* **French Quarter Pasta Salad** *found on page 58, and the* **Mardi Gras Small Dinner Salad***, found on page 101.*)

(*You'll get an ample batch from this recipe with some left over, which won't last long...Enjoy!*)

SAFFRON RICE

Everything You Will Need To Serve 4:

2   tablespoons of butter
1 ½   cups of onion *(chopped)*
1   cup of white rice
¾   teaspoon of Saffron
2   cups of chicken broth

In a sauce pan, melt the butter.

Add the onions and cook for about five or six minutes, or until the onion turns transparent.

Add the rice and Saffron.

Stir the ingredients together until the rice is well mixed with the Saffron.

Add the chicken broth.

Bring to a boil.

Reduce the heat to low and let simmer for twenty to twenty-five minutes, covered.

(Serve this with the **Sausage Sinatra** *found on page 62 or try it with other favorite recipes of your own!)*

RICE PILAF

Everything You Will Need To Serve 4:

2   tablespoons of butter
2   ounces of spaghetti *(broken into thirds)*
1   cup of white rice
2   cups of beef broth

In a sauce pan, melt the butter.

Add the broken spaghetti.

Cook the spaghetti over medium heat for two to three minutes until browned.

Add the rice and beef broth.

Stir and bring to a boil.

Reduce the heat to low and let simmer for twenty to twenty-five minutes, covered.

Serve hot.

(Talk about a perfect match! Try this with **Sausage Kebabs**, *found on page 70.)*

PERFECT WHITE RICE

Everything You Will Need:

4   cups of water
½   teaspoon of salt
1   tablespoon of butter
2   cups of long grain white rice

In a saucepan, bring the water, salt and butter to a boil.

Stir in the rice

Reduce the heat to low and let simmer for twenty to twenty-five minutes, covered *(don't peek!)*.

(Yes, it's perfect, and you'll love it with **Conchipacho**, *found on page 72.)*